AF406112

A TAIL OF TWO HEARTS

Written and Illustrated by Lex Archibald

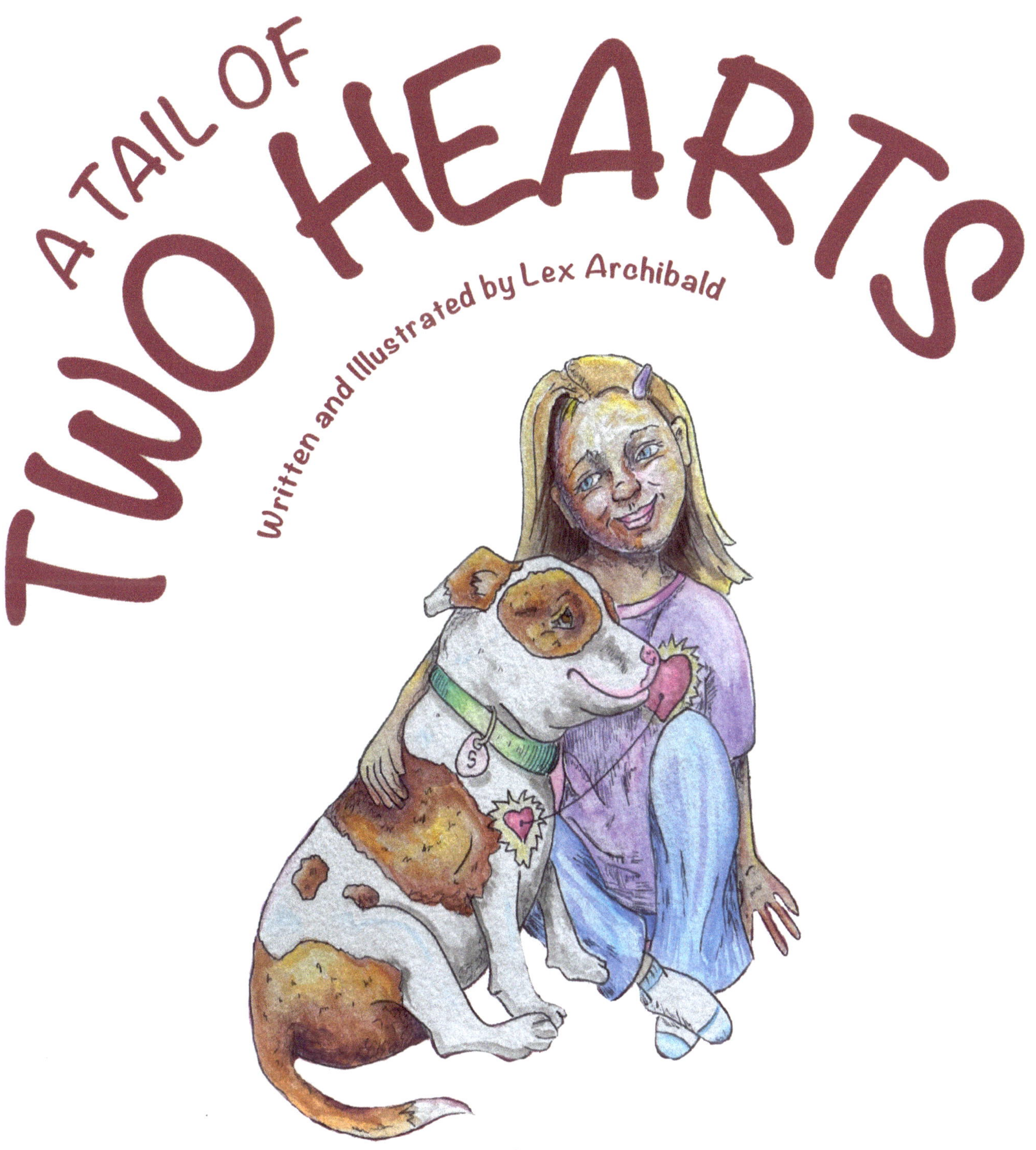

Dedicated to my inspiring and loving muses, Maë and Shoga.

Thank you to all the beautiful pit bulls in the world, and the people who love and advocate for this wonderful breed.

Our rescue pittie, Shoga, is my best friend.
I'll share with you why all the way to the end.
My Shoga girl is a special soul.
Laying her head on Mommy's belly,
knowing her world would soon be whole.

The day arrives and to home I came.
Shoga's eyes lit up, knowing her days wouldn't be the same!
She has a new job besides bathing in the sun.
It is protecting me, lil Maë, her special one.

When I am learning to crawl,
Shoga walks next to me and cheers me on.
She follows me all over as we sing our happy song.

Soon after that, I am standing tall!
Shoga walks behind me, making sure I don't fall.
She helps Mommy clean up the snacks I drop.
It is amazing how her tongue becomes a mop!

Fireworks blast off into the sky.
Shoga is scared, she shakes and lets out a cry.
I hold her tight and pet her head,
helping her stay calm, safe on our bed.

In the dark, I imagine there are monsters out of sight.
Shoga is by my side, helping me get through the scary night.

Taking care of Shoga is a lot of work,
but the love she gives back is the biggest perk.
Giving her the best life I can,
feeding her, walking her, and playing with her,
shows that I'm her biggest fan!

I want to be a veterinarian when I grow up.
Shoga plays along, pretending to be a sick pup.
I check her temp, her paws, and her heart.
You are all better Shoga!
A treat at the end is her favorite part.

Walks for Shoga help her exercise and obey.
When she sees the pond, she hopes we go that way.
She likes to greet her fellow swimming buddies,
wagging her tail and getting her paws all muddy.

When I see a slope, I have to roll down.
Queen of the hill, I earn my crown.
Shoga likes to join in on the fun,
kicking up grass as she rolls and runs.

When it is hot, we go to the water.
Shoga teaches me how to swim like an otter.
The doggie paddle is our secret move.
We splash around and get into our groove.

I love when we explore,
especially when we go to the seashore.
The ocean can be scary--here comes an enormous wave!
Shoga and I look to each other to find our inner brave.

Fall is our favorite time of the year.
I give Shoga some of my clothes to wear.
Spooky and dark on our Halloween walk,
trick or treating around the block.

From the first time we met,
I felt unconditional love.
Our souls fit together like a glove.
Whether we are near or far apart,
we will always be connected at the heart.

Some people think Shoga looks tough and mean,
but love in her heart is all I've seen.
When meeting new people she puts up her paw,
hoping they notice her smile, and not fear her jaw.

Looking at Shoga, she's cuddly and cute.
She's sweet like a pear, my favorite fruit.
She's not scary or mean like some people believe.
So open your mind and let love lead.

Visit a shelter or a rescue,
to find a heart of gold to love you.
A dog will fill your days with such delight,
and your story will make other hearts ignite.

As our tale nears its end,
I bet it's easy to see why Shoga is my best friend.

Now it's time to turn out the light,
kiss and hug my sweet pup goodnight.

As the sky fills with moonlight beams,
Shoga and I wish you a night of sweet dreams.

Zzz

About the author:

Lex is an artist, teacher, mama, and animal advocate with a special place in her heart for pit bulls. The idea to write a book came from the nightly ritual of Lex, Maë, and Shoga piling on the bed for story time. Lex also felt that Maë and Shoga's love story needed to be told to help change the stigma associated with pit bulls.
Maë is a major contributor to the short scenarios in this book.

Animals are gifts to this world; they love unconditionally. Committing to a pet is a big decision that requires a lot of responsibility. But if you do, a love so rich will fill your life.

Choosing where to get your pet is very important. People have a responsibility to help make the lives of animals and pets better. Today, there are many animals, especially pit bulls, that are in overcrowded shelters. Rescue organizations and shelters give animals a second chance at finding a family. They work tirelessly, educate, and advocate, but it takes a collective effort.

Shoga is from It's The Pits, a Southern California rescue organization. Shoga was on the euthanasia list at a shelter and had less than a day to live. It's The Pits brought her to safety, and Lex volunteered to foster Shoga. At first Shoga was shy, terrified of traffic, and very skinny, but she could feel Shoga's desire to trust again. In time, Shoga built confidence, and Lex adopted Shoga seven years ago. Her family cherishes every moment with her.

If you are considering a pet, please reach out to a local shelter or rescue. There are rescue organizations for specific species and breeds.

Remember to adopt, don't shop, and be part of the solution.

Here are some ways to help animals in your community:

- Adopt from a local rescue organization or animal shelter.
- Foster at a rescue/shelter. (All expenses are paid for).
- Sponsor a homeless pet.
- Volunteer at a local rescue/shelter.
- Donate money or needed items to local rescue/shelter.
- Always spay and neuter your pets.